BRITAIN:THE FACTS
Money
Christopher Riches

FRANKLIN WATTS
LONDON•SYDNEY

London Borough of Barnet	
Askews	Jun-2009
332.4941	£12.99

First published in 2008
by Franklin Watts

Design by bounford.com

Franklin Watts
338 Euston Road
London NW1 3BH

Franklin Watts Australia
Level 17/207 Kent Street
Sydney, NSW 2000

ISBN 978 0 7496 8384 9

Dewey classification: 332.4'941

Printed in China

Franklin Watts is a division of Hachette Children's Books,
an Hachette Livre UK company.
www.hachettelivre.co.uk

Picture credits
The publishers would like to thank the following
organisations for their kind permission to reproduce
illustrations in this book:

Cover image: bounford.com

p. 5 Banknotes reproduced by permission of the Bank of
England and the Bank of Scotland; coin designs Crown
Copyright; p. 9 (bottom) Stephanie Schaere, National
Pictures/TopFoto; p. 10 W&N Baker; p. 16 TopFoto/UPPA;
p. 18 (top) TopFoto/World History Archive; p. 19 (bottom)
TopFoto/UPPA; p. 20 (bottom) John Birdsall Social Issues
Photo Library; p. 21 (top) HM Revenue and Customs;
p. 21 (bottom) John Birdsall Social Issues Photo Library;
p. 22 (top) Print Collector/HIP/TopFoto; p. 22 (middle)
Topham Picturepoint/TopFoto; p. 23 (top) PA
Photos/TopFoto; p. 23 (bottom) www.picturenation.co.uk;
p. 24 (top) HIP/TopFoto; p. 25 (top) PA Photos/TopFoto;
p. 25 (bottom) Topham Picturepoint/TopFoto.

All maps, charts and diagrams © bounford.com.

Contents

Our Money

To buy things, we use money –
the pound (£) and the penny (p).
Money also provides a measure of
the value of something.

Where did the £ come from?

The £ sign is in the style of a
handwritten capital letter L with a
crossbar. The L stood for *libra*, a Roman
unit of weight, the origin of the old unit of
weight called the pound. Then 240 pence
weighed a pound, and so that amount of
money was also called a pound. The
symbol £ was used for the money unit
while the symbol lb was used for the weight.

And the penny?

The origin of the penny is
more obscure. Two
theories are:

- It is named after King
  Penda, King of West
  Mercia (in the Midlands)
  who died around 655. He
  helped re-establish the use
  of coins which stopped after
  the Romans left.
- It is named after the pan in which
  the molten metal used to
  produce the coin was held.

What happened before money?

Before there was a system of money people
had to trade one object for another.
This was called **bartering**. You
might trade an hour's labour
for a pint of milk
or exchange a
bucket of
potatoes for a mug
to drink from. In
such a system it is
hard to establish a
value for anything. It is also
hard to trade over any distance.

The penny and
halfpenny used before
decimalisation.

Money slang

There are lots of slang
names for money. Here
are some examples:

£1	quid, nicker, smacker
£5	fiver
£10	tenner
£25	pony
£100	ton
£500	monkey
£1,000	grand

Our money system

Our current decimal system was introduced in 1971. In preparation, the first decimal coins (5p and 10p) started to appear in 1968. Before then there was a system of pounds, shillings and pence (12 pence = 1 shilling; 20 shillings = 1 pound).

There are 100p in £1. The coins have a value of 1p, 2p, 5p, 10p, 20p, 50p, £1 and £2. Notes have the values £5, £10, £20 and £50. The coins were redesigned in 2008. The design of the new coins is based on the Royal Coat of Arms.

Paper money is issued by the Bank of England. The designs have to be very difficult to **forge**. The new £20 note has many features including:

- A metallic thread in the note – hold the note up to the light to see it.

- An image of the Queen's head can be seen when you hold the note up to the light.

- A **holographic** strip with a multi-coloured image of Adam Smith (a famous Scottish economist) and an image that switches between '20' and '£'.

- Various patterns and the figure '20' that appear under **ultraviolet light**.

- When held up to the light a £ sign appears, made up of irregular shapes from both sides of the note.

All in all a lot of effort is put in to making our money secure.

Other notes

In England and Wales, only the Bank of England issues notes. In Scotland and Northern Ireland, the high street **banks** issue their own notes. These notes feature famous people, for example Sir Walter Scott, or typical scenes such as whisky distilleries or Belfast harbour.

Money Around the World

In the past, every country developed its own money system. This can now cause problems when travelling from one country to another. It also makes it difficult for businesses in one country to sell products to another.

The Euro

One idea to make it easier for travelling and trading between countries is to use the same money in different countries. The best example of this is the Euro. The symbol for the Euro is €. This **currency** is used in many European countries. It makes looking after your own money easier, but it can make it difficult for individual countries, as each country has less influence over the value of their currency. This loss of control is the main reason that Britain kept the pound rather than opting for the Euro. The Euro notes are the same throughout Europe. Each country can have its own design on one side of the standard coins.

The Euro zone

The Euro zone describes the countries that use the Euro. From 2009, 16 European Union countries will use the Euro (see below) and 11 will not.

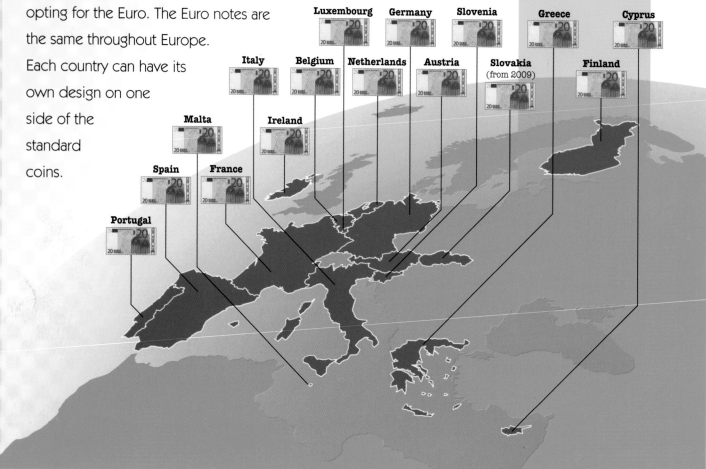

Changing money

How do you change money between different currencies?
The value of a currency is determined by international money markets. The value of different currencies will be reported as:
'Today £1 was worth €1.26.'

If you are going on holiday, you will need to know how much the Euro is worth in pounds, in order to know how much things cost.

To find out: divide £1 by €1.26.
This will tell you that: €1 is worth 79p.

There is a catch with holiday money.
Banks usually charge for changing money from one currency to another.
When the market rate is £1 to €1.26:
a bank may change £1 for €1.21,
and if you bring money back, they may give you £1 for €1.35.

Some currencies are not so easy to convert. On the isolated Pentecost islands in the Pacific island country of Vanuatu, one of the main items used for currency is the pig tusk. The tusks are accepted by the local headteacher to pay for school fees.

Currencies of the world

Nearly every country in the world has its own currency. Countries that use the Euro are one exception. Another is a group of central and west African countries. They use the CFA franc. Important world currencies include:

US dollar ($)	United States of America
Yen (¥)	Japan
Renminbi (RMB)	China
Swiss franc (SFr)	Switzerland
Rupee (Rs)	India
Saudi Arabian Riyal (SR)	Saudi Arabia

The Banking System

We use banks to keep our money safely. Banks also lend money and **invest** money for individuals and companies.

The four largest high street banks in England.

The origins of banking

In 1690, John Freame and Thomas Gould started a banking business in London to help traders. In 1736 they were joined by James Barclay, and they formed the bank we know today as Barclays Bank. There is now quite a choice of banks that provide services to individuals. These banks are sometimes called 'high street banks'. The Bank of England (founded in 1694) does not provide services for individuals. Its special role is described on page 16.

What do banks do?

When you start using a bank, you open a bank account. Your money is put (or **deposited**) into this account. How can you use this money to pay for things?

- You can use a **debit card**. The bank can electronically transfer money from your account to a shop, for example. The card has a microchip that provides details of your account. To authorise the payment you have to enter your PIN (**personal identification number**).This is to make fraud difficult.

- You can use your debit card to get money out of a **cash machine** (an ATM).

- You can write a **cheque**, a special printed form that contains your banking details. You fill this in and it becomes your instruction to the bank to pay money to the person or business named on the cheque.

- You can arrange payments by telephone or **internet banking**.

- Regular payments can be made automatically by the bank if you ask them to make a **direct debit** payment.

Banks provide many other services. They can help you with savings (see pages 10–11) and borrowing (see pages 12–13). The way they provide their services keeps changing. Forty years ago you always had to go to your branch of the bank to obtain money. You had to make special arrangements to take money out of a different branch of the same bank. With cash machines, debit cards and internet banking, it is much easier for us to use a bank's services.

Banks normally (but not always) charge for the services they provide. You will need to check carefully whether you will be charged or not.

A run on the bank

Customers who put their money into a bank have to feel that their money is safe. If a bank makes bad decisions on who it lends money to, it can lose money. Customers then become concerned about their money and so take it out of the bank. As more customers do this, it is called a 'run on the bank'. In 2007 there was a run on the Northern Rock bank because customers no longer felt their money was safe. It is a rare event.

Saving Money

When you have more money than you need, what do you do with it?

Thinking about savings

There are many ways in which you might wish to use your savings. What you do depends on your attitude to **risk**. Look at these three options:

- Putting it in a safe place at home. Its value will not change but it is safe.
- Putting it in a bank's savings account. You will receive **interest** (see below) on that money.
- Buying lottery tickets in the hope of a big win.

The first has virtually no risk but gives you no gain. The last gives the potential of huge gains, but a very high likelihood of loss. Between these two extremes there are many ways to make your savings grow.

Interest

If you lend some of your money to a bank, you receive a payment from them, called interest. Interest is shown as an annual percentage figure. When the rate of interest is 5%, £100 will grow to £105 in one year. Look at the chart. One part shows how £100 will increase over 20 years when 5% interest is paid every year. The second part shows what happens when the interest rate is 10%.

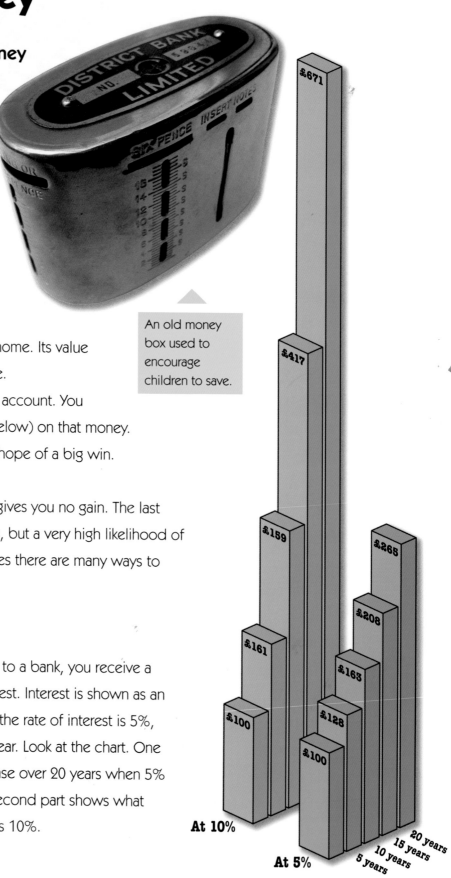

An old money box used to encourage children to save.

£671

£417

£265

£208

£163

£161

£159

£128

£100

£100

At 10%

At 5%

20 years

15 years

10 years

5 years

There are many ways in which you can invest your money and receive regular interest, for example:

- Bank savings or deposit accounts, usually with low levels of interest but with easy access to your funds.
- Independent Savings Accounts (ISAs), special savings accounts where no tax is paid on the interest, unlike other accounts. There are limits on how much can be invested each year.

The stock market

Another way of using your savings is to invest in the **stock market**. The Stock Exchange in London is one of the world's largest stock markets. A stock market is a place where **shares** in companies are traded. A share is just that: a share in the value of a particular company. If the company does well, the value of the share goes up. If it does badly, the value goes down. The company also pays what is called a **dividend** each year. This is a share in the profits of the company. You can invest in the stock market by buying and selling shares. However, the value of stock market investments can go down as well as up, so the investment has some risk.

Stock market jargon

A bear market is when the market goes down and traders are pessimistic. A bear trader is one who sells shares in the hope of buying them again when the price is lower.

A bull market is when the market goes up and the traders are optimistic. A bull trader buys shares in the expectation that their value will rise.

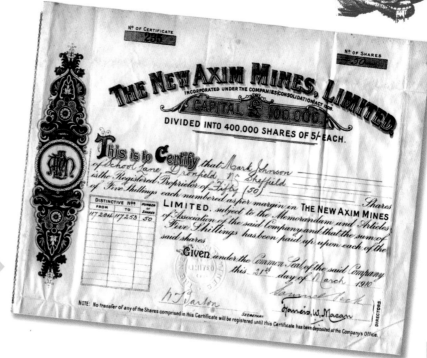

This old share certificate shows that Mark Johnson owned 50 shares in New Axim Mines. Modern certificates look less impressive.

Borrowing Money

When you don't have enough money for an important purchase, it is possible to borrow some. If you borrow some money from your mum, you agree to pay it back as soon as you can. If you borrow from a bank, you have to pay that sum back at regular intervals. You also have to pay interest back to the bank. The interest is the charge the bank makes for lending you the money.

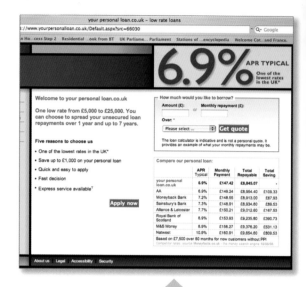

Many companies now offer loans over the internet.

Paying for borrowing money

Normally when you borrow money you agree to pay it back in monthly instalments. This means that each month the amount you owe becomes smaller. As you only pay interest on what you still owe, the amount of that interest gets smaller. When interest charges are shown, they usually have the initials APR after the rate. This stands for **Annual Percentage Rate**, and takes into account the way in which the loan is repaid.

The chart shows the cost of borrowing £1,000 at different interest rates and over different lengths of time. It assumes that repayments are made every month.

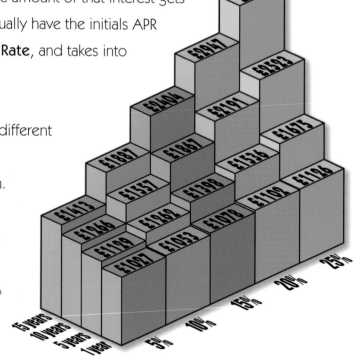

- If you borrowed £1,000 over one year at 5%, the loan will cost you £27 in interest.
- If you borrowed £1,000 over 15 years at 25% interest, the loan will cost you £2,502.

Beware of any loan with a high rate of interest. Sometimes there can be very expensive penalties if payments are not made regularly. Those who offer such loans are called 'loan sharks'.

There are many ways in which money can be borrowed:

- A bank **overdraft**. This is when your bank agrees that you can take out more money than is in your account.

- A personal loan which you agree to pay back on a regular basis.

- A **secured loan** which is also paid back on a regular basis. It will have a lower APR.

- **Credit cards**. With a credit card you can buy something today with the card and pay for it in full within about 30 days or pay for it in monthly payments. If you do the latter you will also pay interest.

Credit cards

- The first credit cards were issued in 1951 by Diners Club, for use by club members in 27 New York restaurants.

- The first British credit card, Barclaycard, was issued in 1966.

- 34 million people in Britain now have credit cards.

- 10 per cent of credit card holders use one every day.

- In 2006, £126 billion was spent using credit cards in the UK.

FACTS

The front side of a typical credit/debit card.

1   Microchip, used when 'Chip and PIN' payment is used. When you place the card in a reader, you enter a four-digit PIN. This is checked against the microchip. If it is correct, the transaction goes ahead. You do not have to sign any authorisation.

2   A hologram for security.

3   A unique 16-digit card number; the first six digits are a code for the bank, the remainder is a personal account code.

4   The expiry date of the card. The card is not valid after this date.

5   Your name.

The reverse side of a typical credit/debit card.

1   The magnetic strip; it contains information about the card that can be read by a magnetic card reader.

2   The place where you sign the card to make it valid.

3   The security code, unique to the card. It is used when the card is used to pay for something over the phone or on the internet.

Paying for Somewhere to Live

Everyone needs somewhere to call home. Most homes are either rented or purchased.

Renting

When you **rent** a house, you are called a **tenant**. You pay the owner (called the **landlord**) a regular weekly or monthly charge called the rent. In most cases the landlord will be responsible for looking after the building. All the terms under which you rent the house are agreed in a formal document called a **lease**. There are three main groups of landlords:

- Local councils, who provide housing for those on low income (**social housing**). Such houses are called council houses.
- Housing associations, who also provide social housing. Increasingly housing associations have taken over the running of council houses.
- Private landlords.

There are laws which regulate rented property.

Buying a house

A house is by far the most expensive purchase anyone makes. The map shows the average price of property in different areas of Britain in early 2008.

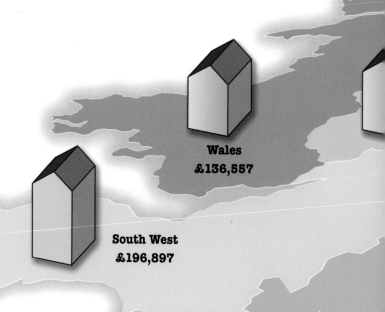

Northern Ireland
£230,000

Wales
£136,557

South West
£196,897

What is a building society?

A building society is owned by its members. Originally you became a member by putting your savings into the society. In turn, the society would then use the savings deposited with it to provide members with loans to purchase houses. The first building society was formed in Birmingham in 1775 by Richard Ketley, at the Golden Cross Inn, Birmingham. There are now 59 building societies in the UK and they are helping over 2 million members buy their own homes.

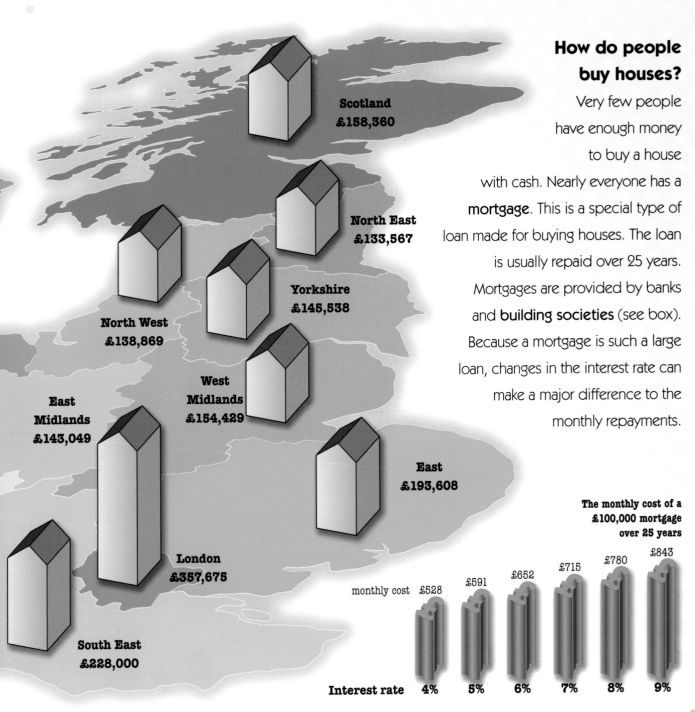

How do people buy houses?

Very few people have enough money to buy a house with cash. Nearly everyone has a **mortgage**. This is a special type of loan made for buying houses. The loan is usually repaid over 25 years. Mortgages are provided by banks and **building societies** (see box). Because a mortgage is such a large loan, changes in the interest rate can make a major difference to the monthly repayments.

Scotland
£158,360

North East
£133,567

Yorkshire
£145,538

North West
£138,869

West Midlands
£154,429

East Midlands
£143,049

East
£193,608

London
£357,675

South East
£228,000

The monthly cost of a £100,000 mortgage over 25 years

monthly cost	£528	£591	£652	£715	£780	£843
Interest rate	4%	5%	6%	7%	8%	9%

The National Economy

The state of the national economy is important for everyone's finances. Its health is strongly influenced by the rate of **inflation**, the level of interest rates and the performance of the stock market.

Inflation

Inflation means that your money will buy less at the end of the year than at the beginning. It happens when the price of goods and services increase. It is measured as the percentage by which prices have increased over a year. The prices of more than 650 different things, including food, energy costs, cinema tickets, holidays, transport costs and electrical and electronic goods, are recorded across Britain. The changes in prices are noted, and the average increase in the price is calculated.

When inflation is high, people suffer because they can buy less with the same money. For example £1 bought around 1 litre of diesel fuel in June 2007 but only 0.75 litres one year later.

The Bank of England

The Bank of England is Britain's national bank and has been so for over 300 years. It fixes the interest rate it charges to lend money to high street banks. They, in turn, use this to calculate their interest rates for borrowers and savers. The Bank of England uses the interest rate to control inflation and to keep the financial market stable. Key activities of the Bank of England include:

- Fixing the interest rate.
- Managing the value of the pound.
- Issuing bank notes.
- Looking after Britain's gold reserves.
- Acting as the government's banker.

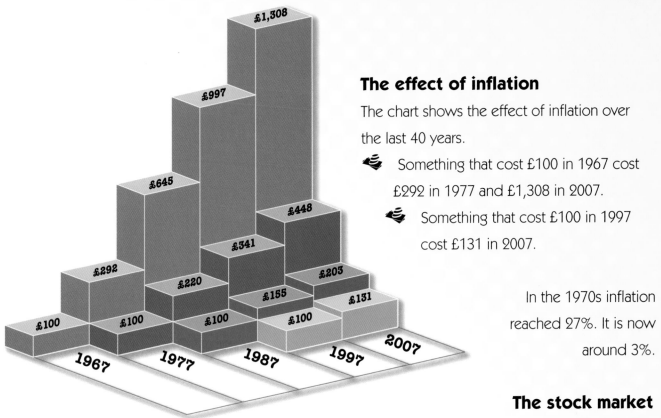

The effect of inflation

The chart shows the effect of inflation over the last 40 years.

- Something that cost £100 in 1967 cost £292 in 1977 and £1,308 in 2007.
- Something that cost £100 in 1997 cost £131 in 2007.

In the 1970s inflation reached 27%. It is now around 3%.

The stock market

The movement of prices on the stock market (see page 11) provides a guide to the health of the economy. The performance is most commonly measured by the *Financial Times* FTSE 100 index. It records the price movements in the shares of Britain's 100 largest companies. The Index changes every day. The chart below shows its movements in one month. Over a long period of time the stock market will increase in value. In the short term, it can go up and down a lot.

Taxes

It has been said that there are only two things in life that are certain – death and **taxes**. Governments raise taxes to pay for the services they provide to their citizens. Some taxes are paid directly by individuals while others are paid indirectly, for example by taxing the things we buy.

Direct taxes

The most well-known direct tax is **income tax**. This is a tax on the money an individual earns from working or from investments.

How income tax works

- You are able to earn a certain amount before you pay any tax.
- In the 2008–9 tax year, you can earn £6,035 free of tax.
- From £6,036 to £40,835, you pay 20% of your earnings in tax.
- Above £40,835, you pay 40%.

If you are working, your employer takes the tax off your earnings and pays it direct to the government. This system is called Pay-As-You-Earn (PAYE). Each employee has a tax code which HM Revenue and Customs, the government department that collects tax, has calculated.

This is to ensure that your tax payments take account of your 'personal allowance' of £6,035 tax-free income and any other allowance or charge that is personal to you.

As well as paying tax on earned income, you also have to pay tax on income from investments and from rents.

Other direct taxes

- National Insurance (see page 20), payable at the rate of 11% of income between £5,435 and £40,040.
- Inheritance tax is paid on the wealth of someone who has died. The tax, at 40%, is paid on total wealth valued in excess of £312,000. In some circumstances tax will only be paid on wealth valued above £624,000.

Indirect taxes

Direct taxes are paid on the money we receive. **Indirect taxes** are paid on things we decide to do or need. Some examples are:

- Value Added Tax (VAT). On nearly everything we buy, 17.5% of the price is tax, which the retailer passes to the government. Food, children's clothes and shoes, public transport and newspapers and books are the main items not taxed in this way.
- Excise duties are paid on alcoholic drinks, cigarettes, petrol and diesel.
- Air passenger duty is paid by everyone flying out of a UK airport.

Calculating take-home pay in 2008-9		
1	Total pay for year	£17,500.00
2	Personal allowance	£6,035.00
3	Taxable income (1 – 2)	£11,465.00
4	Tax paid (20% of 3)	£2,293.00
National Insurance paid on £12,065 (£17,500 – £5,435, the NI threshold)		
5	11% of £12,040	£1,327.15
6	Total tax and NI (4 + 5)	£3,620.15
7	Take-home pay (1 – 6)	£13,879.85

A receipt showing that no VAT is charged on books.

```
YOUR RECEIPT
THANK YOU
19/06/2008 10:23
000001#1420 CLERK 01      01

BOOKS
SUBTOTAL           £1.50
INC VAT@0%         £1.50
0% VAT =           £1.50
                   £0.00

ITEMS
CASH        £1. 50
```

You pay a special tax when you fly from a UK airport.

National Insurance and the Benefit System

Paying National Insurance entitles you to certain benefits. The government provides other benefits independent of your National Insurance payments.

What is National Insurance?

National Insurance is paid by everyone who is in work and who is earning above a certain level (in 2008, £105 a week). Employers also contribute for every person they employ.

When you are given a National Insurance number, you will receive a card like this with your own name and number on it.

National Insurance number

You will normally receive a National Insurance number shortly before your 16th birthday. Everyone has their own unique number. This number is used throughout the benefits and tax system. The number consists of two letters followed by six numbers and then ending in a letter, for example AB-12-34-56-D.

National Insurance benefits

The following are the main benefits. The amount you receive is based on how much National Insurance you have paid:

- A state **pension** (see page 22).
- Jobseeker's Allowance, a weekly payment when you are out of work and looking for a job. Payment is reviewed after six months.
- Incapacity benefit, a weekly payment if you are unable to work as a result of an injury or ill-health.

Benefit payments can help support someone looking for work.

Other benefits

The state pays out benefits to a wide range of people. Some of these benefits, such as child benefit, are called universal. These are benefits that are paid to everyone that is entitled to them. Other benefits are **means-tested**, which means that they are paid only to people who can show that their income is below a certain figure.

Child benefit

This is paid to the parent or guardian of every child under 16 and those under 19 who are at school or studying at an equivalent level at college. It is paid because it is recognised that bringing up children is expensive. The weekly benefit paid in 2008 for a first child is £18.80 and for other children £12.55.

A leaflet that explains how to claim child benefit.

Benefits for those on low incomes

There are a range of benefits for those on low income that provide assistance with housing costs, for example. These benefits are means-tested.

Applying for child tax credit will bring more money to help bring up the children.

Tax credits

Another way of providing benefits has been used since 2003. You can claim child **tax credit** if you are a parent and working tax credit if you are on a low income. Working tax credit can help with child care costs. You have to apply for the credits, and then they will be paid monthly.

Pensions

People still need money to live on when they stop work. When you work you save money so that you can receive a pension when you **retire**.

Retirement age

- In 1946 pensions were paid when a man reached 65 and a woman reached 60. These became the ages at which people stopped work (or retired).
- At that time a man was expected to live until 64 and a woman until 68.
- Now a boy born in 2006 is expected to live until 77 and a girl until 81.
- In stages between 2010 and 2020, the retirement age for women is being increased from 60 to 65.
- Then there will be a gradual increase in retirement age to 68 for both men and women by 2046.

Pensioners collecting their pension at a post office.

- In 2006 the average age at which men retired was 64.2 years; for women it was 61.8 years.
- In 2005 only 39% of the working population were in a company or private pension scheme.
- 4.7 million people are not saving enough for their retirement.

The state pension

The state pension was introduced in 1909 by the Liberal Chancellor of the Exchequer, David Lloyd George (above). A weekly pension of between 10p and 25p was paid to those aged 70 or over if their income was below a certain figure. It was introduced to stop old people having no money to live on. In 1946 a compulsory scheme to which everyone contributed was introduced. The size of the pension paid depended on the number of contributions made. This remains the basis of the system today.

Other support for pensioners

The government also provides a range of other benefits, such as the winter fuel payments to help pensioners to keep warm in winter, and free bus transport. In total 59% of the benefits budget is spent on helping pensioners.

Pensioners campaigning for an increased pension.

The state pension is set at a fairly low level. In 2008 it was £90 a week for a single person and £145 for a couple. If you want to have more in your retirement, you will have to save for a pension. The government is keen for people to do this and encourages various schemes, including stakeholder pensions.

A stakeholder pension is a simple form of personal pension that was established with government support.

Company pensions

Most employers are required to provide a pension scheme for employees to take part in, and most of them will make a contribution to these pension plans along with contributions from employees. It is a good way of saving. There are a number of different schemes. A final-salary scheme provides a pension based on a person's salary at retirement. A personal pension is one where you save money that is then used to provide you with a pension when you retire.

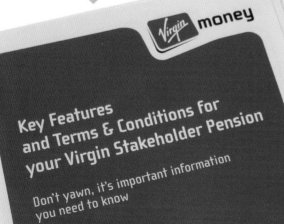

Virgin money

Key Features and Terms & Conditions for your Virgin Stakeholder Pension

Don't yawn, it's important information you need to know

Insurance

What happens if your home is burgled? If you are insured, the insurance company will pay for the stolen goods to be replaced. If you are not insured, you will have to pay for replacements yourself. You have to spend money on **insurance** while you hope you will never have to use it.

How does insurance work?

Taking a house as an example, you need to insure the building against damage, from a fire, for example. You will also want to insure all the contents against damage, loss or theft.

You provide details of what you want to insure to the insurance company. They work out a **premium** (the annual amount they will charge) based on a number of factors, such as where you live, the type of house, the value of the contents and the security of the house. If the house burns down, you make a **claim** to the insurance company. After they have accepted the claim, they will pay for the rebuilding of the house.

Important areas of insurance include:

- Life insurance. You can insure your life so that, if you die, the insurer will pay out money to your family.

When did insurance start?

In 1666 the Great Fire of London burnt down over a third of the houses in London. After the fire, people began to think of ways of reducing the financial risk of owning a house. The first person to offer insurance against fire was Nicholas Barbon (he was originally named Hath-Christ-Not-Died-For-Thee-Thou-Wouldst-Be-Damned but preferred to be known as Nicholas). By 1680 he had established 'The Fire Office', Britain's first insurer. The Fire Office also founded the first fire brigade – but it would only put out fires in houses insured by the Fire Office.

An insurance company used to fix a sign like this to a house to show that it was insured by them.

Car insurance will help pay for the damage caused in a car crash.

- Car insurance. It is against the law not to insure a car. Premiums are particularly high for young drivers. Insurance companies look at their records of claims and know that young people are more likely to have an accident.

- Health insurance. Insurance that entitles you to certain levels of treatment by private doctors or dentists.

- Travel insurance. This covers you while you are travelling, with particular emphasis on medical cover and for emergency changes in travel plans.

This card entitles you to a certain level of medical treatment in Europe.

Holidays should be perfect. Travel insurance is there to protect you against the unexpected.

Believable claims?

To claim money from an insurer you have to explain what happened. Here are some unlikely animal stories told to the Norwich Union insurance company:

'A zebra collided with my car when I was at a safari park.'

'A frozen squirrel fell out of a tree and crashed through the windscreen on to the passenger seat.'

'The car was parked when a reindeer fell on the bonnet of my car.'

'A herd of cows licked my car and caused damage to the paintwork.'

'A cow jumped on my quad bike.'

A Household Budget

How do all these financial issues actually affect you? It is always important that you have more money than you spend. As life becomes more complex, it becomes all the more important to know about the state of your finances.

Making a budget

A **budget** is a way of looking at the amount of money you expect to receive, and the amount of money you spend. You hope that you will receive more than you spend, so you can save some money. If you are spending more than you earn, you will need to cut back on spending or you will need to pay to borrow some money.

Spending

There are a lot of things you can spend money on. Once you have children to support and a house to look after, the importance of managing your money becomes even greater.

Typical areas of spending include:

- Paying for somewhere to live (rent or mortgage payment).
- **Council tax** payment on your home.
- Electricity, gas and water bills.
- Phone, internet and television costs.
- Food and clothing.
- Eating out, leisure activities and holidays.
- Travel to work and other transport costs, including running a car.
- House, car and other insurance.
- Savings and borrowings.

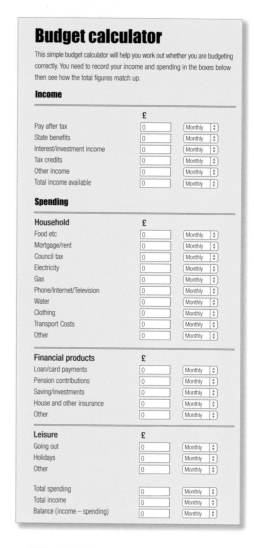

Typical household bills for Council tax, electricity and gas.

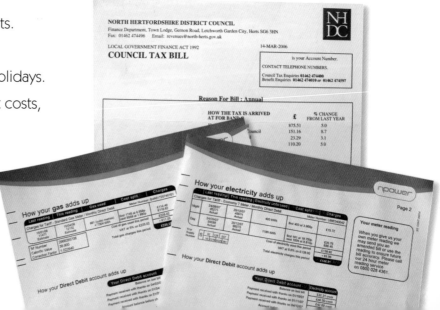

Income

The money you receive may come from various sources:

- Money from working (remember that an employer has to deduct tax and National Insurance before you see the money).
- Interest and other investment income.
- Benefit payments (for example, child benefit, housing allowance).
- Tax credits.
- Gifts.

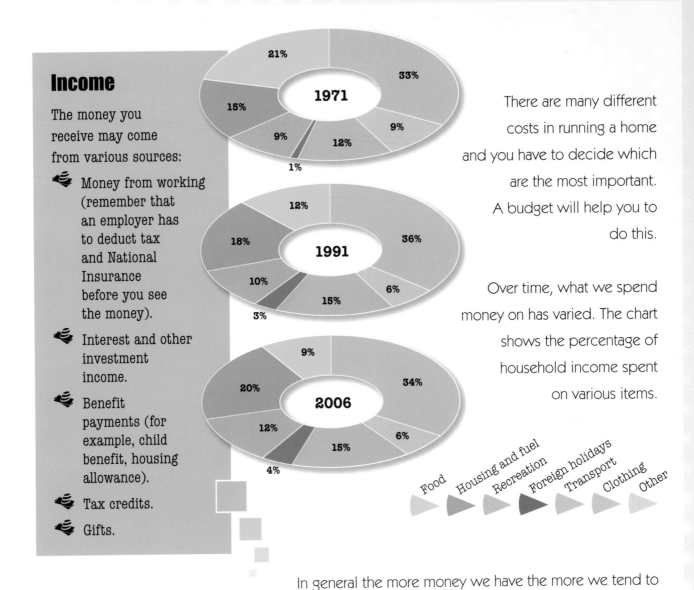

There are many different costs in running a home and you have to decide which are the most important. A budget will help you to do this.

Over time, what we spend money on has varied. The chart shows the percentage of household income spent on various items.

Food   Housing and fuel   Recreation   Foreign holidays   Transport   Clothing   Other

In general the more money we have the more we tend to spend. Look at the figures below for the weekly expenditure in three types of household, taken from a national expenditure survey.

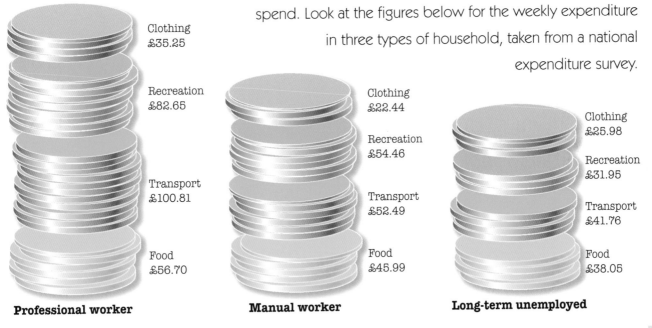

Professional worker

Clothing £35.25
Recreation £82.65
Transport £100.81
Food £56.70

Manual worker

Clothing £22.44
Recreation £54.46
Transport £52.49
Food £45.99

Long-term unemployed

Clothing £25.98
Recreation £31.95
Transport £41.76
Food £38.05

Discussion Points

Here are a few suggestions for discussion points on all the different aspects of money that have been covered (the page numbers indicate where a topic appears in the book).

- What are the advantages and disadvantages of a bartering system? Can you think why governments do not like such systems (think about taxes)? (**page 4**)

- Should Britain stop using the pound and start using the Euro? (**page 6**)

- If you had £10,000, how would you invest it? Think about your attitude to risk. (**page 10**)

- Look at the cost of borrowing money shown on **page 12**. Why do you think it is important only to borrow money when you can manage to repay it regularly?

- Why do you think house prices in different parts of Britain vary so much? (**page 14**)

- Which of the taxes described on **pages 18–19** do you think is most fair and which is least fair?

- Why should a government pay benefits to people? (**page 20**)

- What would it be like if old people did not receive a pension? Find out what it would have been like one hundred years ago. (**page 22**)

- Why do you think insurance is described as something you spend money on in the hope of never having to use it? (**page 24**)

- Try making a budget for one month of your own spending. (**page 26**)

Websites

There are a number of sites designed to introduce you to money matters:
www.learnaboutmoney.org/
http://money.citizenshipfoundation.org.uk/
www.moneymatterstome.co.uk/

The Money Matters to Me site has a useful selection of interactive workshops (including a cash machine simulator). Find out more at:
www.moneymatterstome.co.uk/Interactive-Workshops/default.htm

To find out more about how the economy works visit the Bank of England education site Pounds and Pennies. This address takes you to a listing of information cards:
www.bankofengland.co.uk/education/poundsandpence/information.htm

HM Treasury has an introductory website:
www.redbox.gov.uk/

To find our more about the coins we use and their history, visit the Royal Mint site. The Royal Mint is responsible for all our coins. The first address gives details of our current coins and how they are made. The second address gives more on the history of our coinage:
www.royalmint.gov.uk/Corporate/British Coinage/british_coinage.aspx
www.royalmint.gov.uk/Corporate/Museum/orginsofthemuseum.aspx

For information on banknotes, visit the Bank of England site. The best place to start is this virtual tour of our banknotes:
www.bankofengland.co.uk/banknotes/virtualtour/virtual_tour_flash.htm

To find out about banknotes in Scotland visit the Committee of Scottish Clearing Bankers. On this page there are links to the designs for individual banks and a poster containing all Scottish banknotes:
www.scotbanks.org.uk/banknote_denominations.php

There is no similar page for Northern Ireland. The websites of individual banks will have details.

To see the effects of inflation, the Bank of England has an online inflation calculator that calculates back to 1750:
www.bankofengland.co.uk/education/inflation/calculator/flash/index.htm

The Financial Services Authority has a site for young adults providing a lot of information on personal finance called What About Money:
www.whataboutmoney.info/

They also have an adult information site that is designed to be jargon free:
www.moneymadeclear.fsa.gov.uk/

For official information on taxes and benefits, visit the government website:
www.direct.gov.uk/en/moneytaxandbenefits

Note to parents and teachers: Every effort has been made by the Publishers to ensure that these websites are suitable for children, that they are of the highest educational value, and that they contain no inappropriate or offensive material. However, because of the nature of the Internet, it is impossible to guarantee that the contents of these sites will not be altered. We strongly advise that Internet access is supervised by a responsible adult.

Glossary

Annual Percentage Rate (APR) The way in which interest rates are stated so that consumers can more easily compare different rates.

bank A business that keeps people's money. It also lends money and provides other services.

bartering A kind of trading where one item or service is exchanged for another without using money.

budget A plan to show how much money you expect to receive and how much you plan to spend over a given period.

building societies Societies that lend money to their members to buy houses.

cash machine A machine that lets you take cash out of your account at any time. Its formal name is an Automated Teller Machine (ATM).

cheque A specially printed form that allows you to tell the bank who to pay money to. You have to sign a cheque to make it valid. Their use is declining as more banking is done electronically.

claim A request to an insurance company to pay you for a loss, for example, when something has been stolen.

council tax A tax raised by local councils to pay for services such as refuse collection and upkeep of roads. Its size depends on the value of your home.

credit card A plastic card with a microchip that is accepted as a way of paying for things, for example, in shops or restaurants. You pay money to the credit card company later. If you do not pay the full amount, you will be charged interest.

currency The money system used by a country. Our currency is the pound.

debit card A plastic card with a microchip that is accepted as a way of paying for things, for example, in shops or restaurants. The money is taken directly from your bank account.

deposit To put money into a bank or some form of savings.

direct debit An instruction from you to a bank to make regular payments to another organisation.

dividend A payment made by a company to those who own shares in that company.

forge To make an illegal copy of something and to persuade people that it is genuine.

holographic Describing an image that looks different at different angles.

income tax A tax paid on the money you earn from work or investments.

indirect taxes Taxes which you pay when you spend your money, for example, Value Added Tax (VAT).

inflation The percentage increase in the price of goods and services over a given time period.

insurance A way you can pay for financial protection against things you do not want to happen. You can insure against your possessions being stolen, for example.

interest The amount of money you receive as payment for investing your savings or the amount of money you pay as a charge for borrowing money.

internet banking Arranging your banking via a secure internet link rather than by visiting a branch. It makes keeping your finances under control easier.

invest To put money into a bank or a company with the aim of increasing its value.

landlord The owner of a property that is rented.

lease A legal document that you sign when you rent a property.

means-tested Checking if you are entitled to receive a benefit that is only available to those whose income is less than a particular amount.

mortgage A special loan used for buying a house.

overdraft An agreed amount you can borrow from a bank.

pension A regular payment made to people who have retired.

personal identification number A four-digit code that only you know which identifies you as the owner of a credit or debit card.

premium The annual amount you pay to an insurance company for its protection.

rent The amount paid to a landlord for the use of a flat or house.

retired To describe when a person stops working because of his or her age.

risk Uncertainty or danger.

secured loan A loan of money at a lower rate of interest because it is linked to something you own, particularly a house. If you do not repay the loan, the person who has lent you the money can make you sell your house to obtain his money.

share An investment of a fixed size in a company – a share of the value of the company.

social housing Rented housing provided by local government or housing associations rather than private landlords. They consider the needs of the tenant, not just the ability to pay the rent.

stock market A financial market where shares are traded.

tax credit A system of payments to those on low incomes or with children designed to help the least well off.

taxes The payments a government requires of its citizens in order to pay for the services provided.

tenant A person who rents a property from a landlord.

ultraviolet light A colour of light we cannot normally see. When a banknote is placed under an ultraviolet light it looks different, and this can help protect us against forged banknotes.

Index